HOMINID LEAP

BY 1ST 5TH

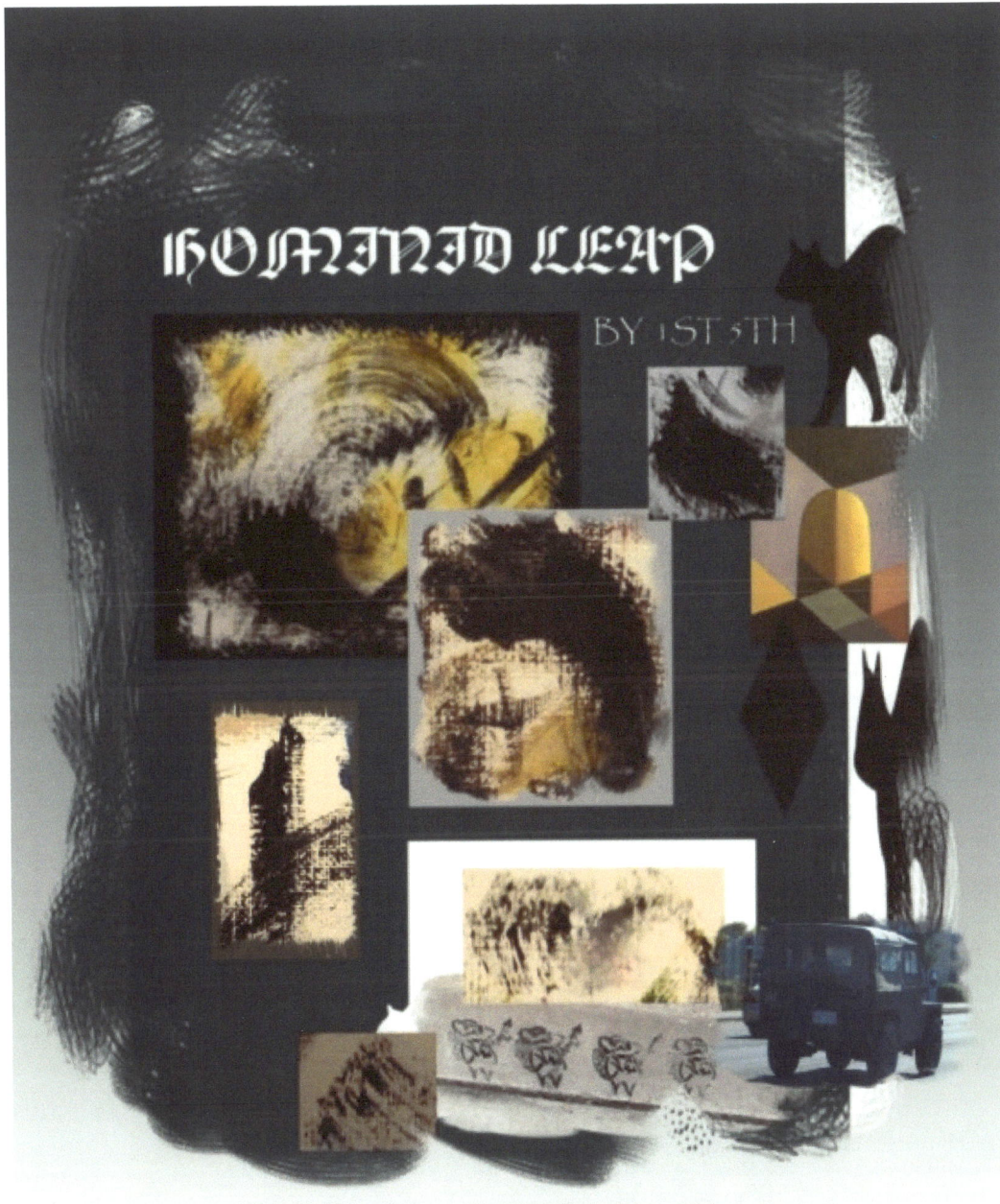

ISBN # 9780981326177 Copyright © 1st 5th 2011   www.nuts4mars.com

Sky Trails by CF-18 Hornets & Cdn Jet Liners Edmonton, Alberta, Canada Quantum Psi /Phantom Ops 1st 5th

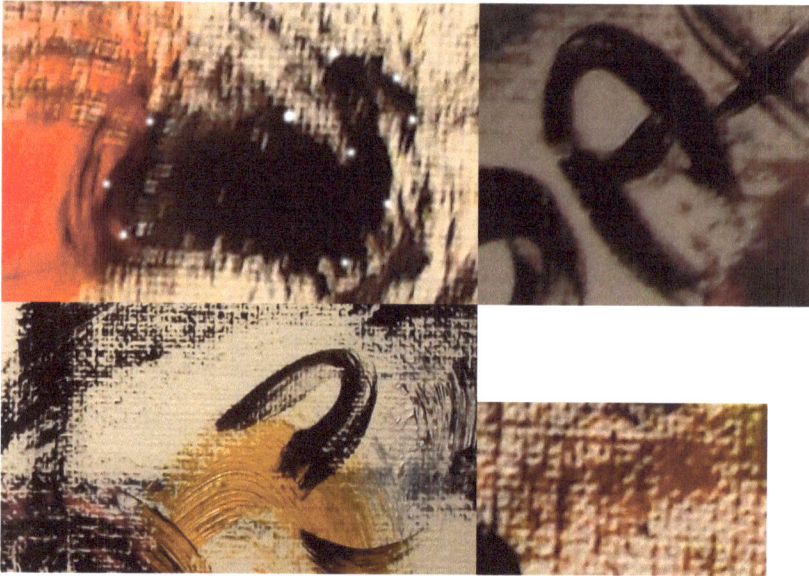

Authentic Desert Rats (USA Marines) RV: Row of camels with tip of scope

So they have a new tv show it's called 'so what did Charley say today?' fighting for our Freedoms

He said 'lick my feet' to cbs...

NO ! NOT CHARLEY II

Piranha (movie) and Remote View painting Feb 27/11

USS KEARSARGE   on top of it all

NECRO HO PREDICTION: EAT THE RICH FIRST

In the movie, I AM LEGEND (starring Will Smith) they ate each other the ones that survived. It was part of the post apocalyptic days script. They cannibalized ..not just some going into monster ghoul mode. It's Africa they mightT (uncanny how that looks like a menu huhT.)

British Royal Prince William & fiance Kate Middleton; Ancient Egyptian Hieroglyph 'hen'
USS REAGAN black broom & above emote; assist to Japan after 8.9 quake & tsunami 2011

STAR TRAIL The Mars Claim - HOOPLA TO SOME SHEER DESTINY TO OTHERS

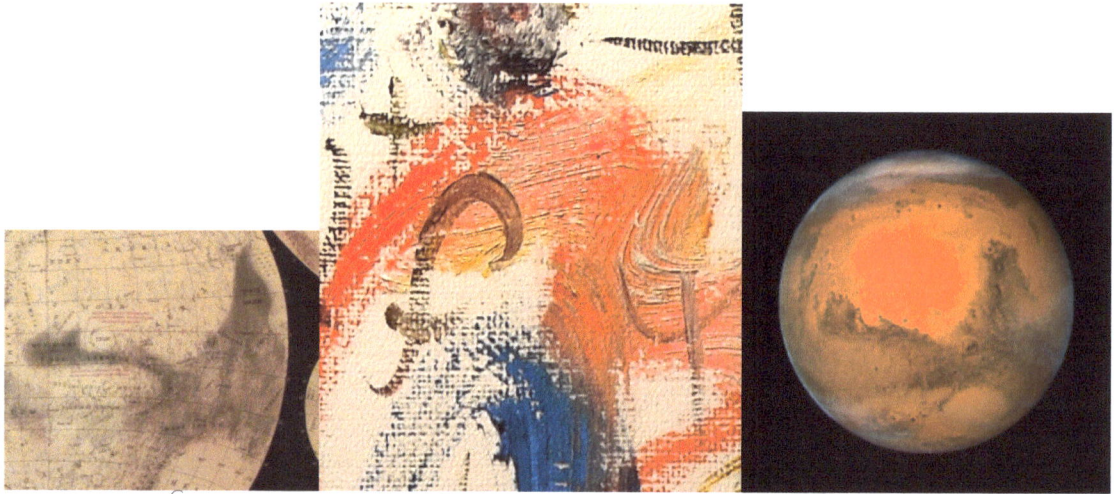

MAP of Mars with RV color match & time synch (see Necro Ho for links to Detectives Starsky & Hutch)

As determined by Sovereign Queen of Mars, 1st 5th by prior Psi Claim

- (see details in *Knights of Mars* by 1st 5th free ebook links on homepage www.nuts4mars.com)

written RV as a streaming account, during the original discovery of the Quantum Star Trail developed further as OPEN STARGATE/Q5Leap/Phantom Ops. Includes Mars Claim paints/psi.

Sovereign bequeathed title to Knights of Mars - (National Geographic Map 1973)

Divisions of the Planet Mars to the Earth's Military, & Law Enforcements

Title to -Air Forces- territory (Map center orb) above the Equator and equidistant Left/Right of Central Meridian, Crater 86 to Crater 91, THARSIS to EDEN/ARABIA inclusive.
First Rock: Achilles Pons.

To- Police/law enforcement- below the Equator and to the Left/Right of the Central Meridion with ARGYREI inclusive.
First Rock: Crater 44.

To- ARMY- (Map center orb) the area AMAZONIS left to XANTHE right. Above the equator and equidistant both left and right of the Meridian.
First Rock: Volcano 12.

To- NAVY- area above the equator and equidistant both left and right of the Meridian (Map's 3rd orb) AERIA to AMAZONIS.
First Rock: Crater 54.

To- MARINES - HELLAS, First Rock - Crater 29 at top.

To- SEALS - ELYSIUM, First Rock - Volcano 8

With a cool *First Rock- Crater One* for the Quantum Viewer 1st 5th & to
Ingo Swann *First Rock* - largest Volcano in the Solar System, Olympus Mons.

Map surface of Mars has a Shadow visual of a Flag. Now that's overlap territory, so it's both the Air Force & the Army & further the Navy; and Law and Marines, as they merge together there is no one line for distinction. Mars territories have zones of overlap where others can comfortably assimilate and there is not the abrupt division like the early Earth.

* *Additionally, with Land for Phantom Ops valour performed by (Fmr) SEAL Charlie Sheen.*

WAIT THESE SHEEP HAVE TEETH!!   Vampire Sheep

Blade starring Wesley Snipes - Vampires & Garlic

Wesley Snipes profile Quantum Psi painting

French - Libya no fly zone 1st strike - 4 of Gaddafi's tanks

USS Stout & USS Whitney - Libya no fly zone TOMAHAWK CRUISE MISSILES

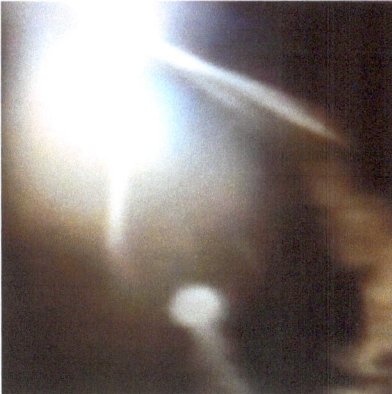

British submarine Remote View psi painting; fired two missiles on Gaddafi's compound March 2011

CANADIAN FIGHTER JET - Libya no fly zone 2011

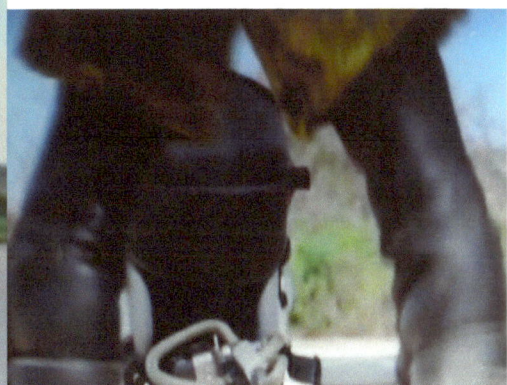

I ROBOT starring Will Smith

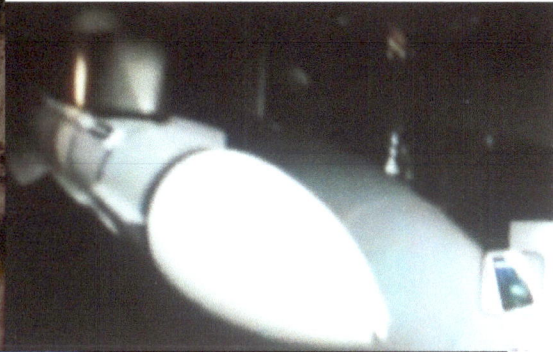

USA Fighter Jet Pilots

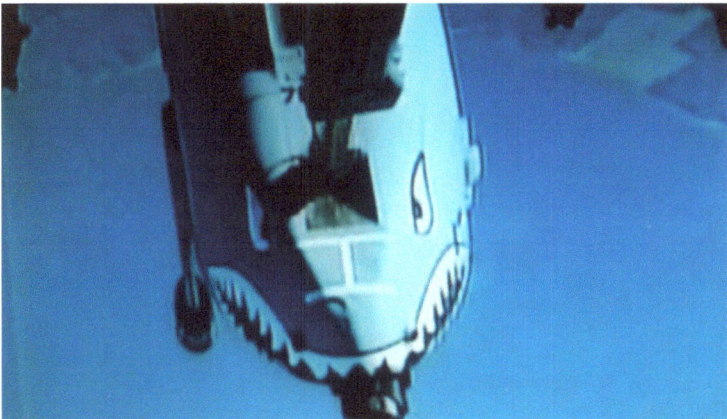

Libya liberation

All trails have PLODDING involved.

That's like a **STAR TRAIL** *WARNING*

{in progress}... **So I said** *PROBABLY* **in a tent , hiding in the desert, or he would be out speaking; and there he was all ready to just jump in for the T. T. Photo rave ops**

NOW he* is in the desert T. Where he is 'safe' from some fool actually Martyring him.

*gaddaf, Libya's loony

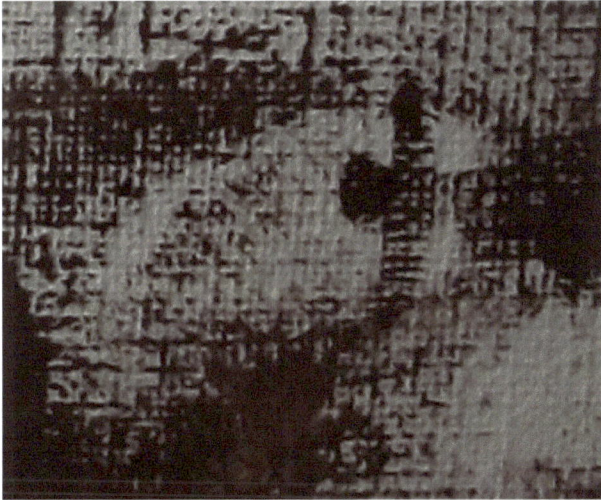

Air Force 'ET' moment, Libya 2011

UK Libya assist 2011

Movie 'FREEZE' wolves; broken bone (upper)
This is a work in progress we add to it constantly…

comedy NECRO HO link homepage www.nuts4mars.com

Shoot them on sight comes to mind…

oh just looking into the FUTURE

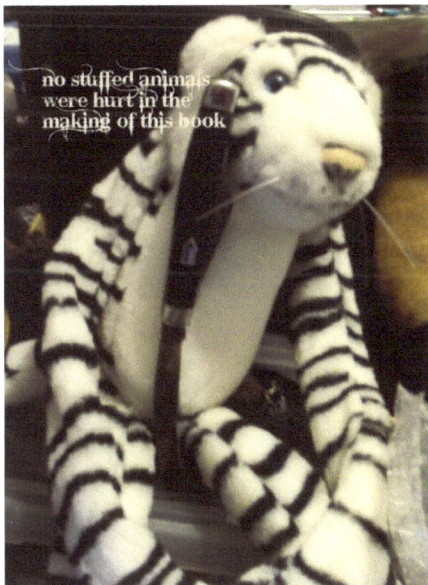

no stuffed animals were hurt in the making of this book

I DON'T DO ECUMENICAL I DO THIS.   IN   the knife between the balls

new movie action comedy RED starring Bruce Willis and a cast of All Stars …(yes, that was actually my psi I 'shot' the action still and then we watched RED….good one!

ANARCHY BROKEN LIQOUR STORE WINDOWS YAHOOS WITH BOOZE!!!! DEAD CRASH-APE/Youth ALL OVER *shame….. littering*

POETRY FROM THE DEAD ALL OVER BUT STILL HERE ZOINE

Hey- if you can't stand some typing you won't make it out anywhere near the sheer UNKNOWN of the Deepside Exploration happening at an Open Quantum Stargate.

So far all the enemy has attained is a desert mirage consisting of
FASTER THEY WIN THE SOONER THEY LOSE
Like the relentless fate of sand in an hourglass.

Stardate 3478

'swann is growing ever creepier..'

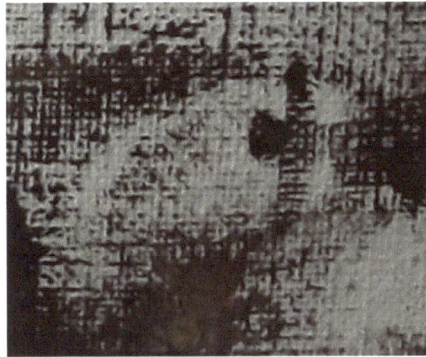

RV - movie ET

Quantum Stargate RVpaints/script link to significant events/objects concerned with a particular security issue or earthly developments and occurrence. As Quantum Psi travels it, the trail has a time arrow that can go backwards and forwards. Along this trail we experience an effect called PATTERN RECOGNITION. Often the Psi will link up in precog fashion to an upcoming presentation of object or other sense item match; of no substantial importance in and of themselves. Considered 'pebbles' as such, but if there are enough of them outstanding in some particular time frame, like coloured pebbles that stand out at the side of the road they might figure in. But mostly that's what it is merely a repeated PATTERN RECOGNITION and not the focus of concern.
There is also Precision Visuals, Timesynch and other wondrous deeds involved!

The car is travelling the highway independent of the pebbles along the trail, they are part of it, but not any significant meaning like 'o I passed by 89000 pebbles today' or gosh there sure were a lot of pebbles and man they all looked the same must mean we are to stay the same…it's NOT like that. But that said a great part of what we do here with the Codes (trained psi/pixel links takes years to learn) And Quantum Leap for security is read the emotes and RV theme encapsulations for their message content, like holistic info packets. Most often they are **DESCRIPTIVE** and also often enough with a ***directional Necker Cube shift***; that's what we try to decode for tips and clues, security aids.

I DO REAL RECONNAISSANCE I was not making that up. It's what it was called all during training MRO and it's what I do.

Reconnaissance is a form or branch of Spying …. And it's every bit as much demanding and comprehensive.

That is a drain in libya like over here the drain they take on your resources and time and effort. They set up for that….they mess up YOUR supplies and YOUR strength and patience and work and ….

They deliberately aim for that. But that said until you shut them down at the base of their ability to form conflict you will have to stave them off but that's not a permanent condition they want to end it satisfactorily not just RUN or SURRENDER I read you that you run when YOU are in control not when they force you to because you let them overwhelm you …that was I Ching advisement they know that shit…. Good advise to listen to. Confusious wore out a copy … ORACLE is for that and I am pretty open … I just receive impressions I am certainly NOT any Goddess 'creating or manifesting' this is NOT a 'makie matter machine' that's just the silly savages ideas… ok so maybe swann eats toast.. That is still pattern recog and perhaps a dot to 'food concerns' and the USS ships that they toast with bottle breaking ceremonies… celebrate, toast… sure these are nice for that too I like to add things in the books to commemorate them, to add to their tales the books format can be entirely reworked it's the collection I wouldn't have it if I just kept boxes of them with out the photo catch… it's essential. Like SUN & EARTH for our life form. You seem to fail to realize that distinction. You take earth shove it out there you are not going to make it ., we are sun forms on a dirt form … and our form requires both.

You will go further on the path of advancements when you keep an open mind and are able to adapt and tweak conceptually … the more accurate the understanding of the basics our foundations and the better we are for getting a boost along the way …

SUN FORMS… humans. Inseparable? They live underground … some… for long periods but sun forms vs. earth forms? Interesting concept. Light beings dark beings…. And if they go deep in the water and made colonies? More deep dark beings. Sun to dark is another descriptive for interstellar cruises IF you took the long form of travel for parts of a trip.

For the tourist view what else.

Well they would both be creatures IN the light and then the others IN the dark. So the 'what condition surrounds' to be IN is the

Are they light if they are a ship with it's lights on but surrounded by light years of dark appearance? Is that a Dark Being, but with a dot of light on, perhaps.

Seeing the psyche as extending out and being defined or determined by the surrounding circumstances, like the original physical extension of the Sun's Light being the descriptive for Sun Light Humans on Earth not the 'we go into dark rooms or dark periods' you see. So there would still be a dark form and light form as the central or main factor the Condition of the entity; in order to make the discernment between dark & light.

Duchess Kate 2011 hat and crown

Easy I can stand in line backwards kinda with the stapler up 'as if it's stuck and I am fixing it' ...

Works for me.

Anybody gets body parts in too close I do a **OOPS I was just going to shake a staple free you must have blah blahT**

...and too much more flack I can always add a paper saying **LOSER** ...

Just working on a few 'g__ assaults issues' mankind has a few Neanderthal genes that did NOT get out of the shallow end yet .... Wait until the whips chains and bare ass crew want their

Rights and Proper Respect in grocery lines now there is a match for the Burkas with Rights and lots-of-cloth-for-ad-displays gang...

(what was the name of Simpson's Burns' sidekick ... that guy....)

No way! That's not the New Order World

logo is it!

Psi paint June 8, 2011, hat brim & braid of new Edmonton Police Chief Knecht.

Tribute to missing Edm Cop Ronnie Chiu

Canadian Leopard Tanks *returning to Base, Afghanistan; 'black panther' swoop emote, as an RV descriptive for 'leopard=cat=panther', with dark black wide streak visual psi paint*

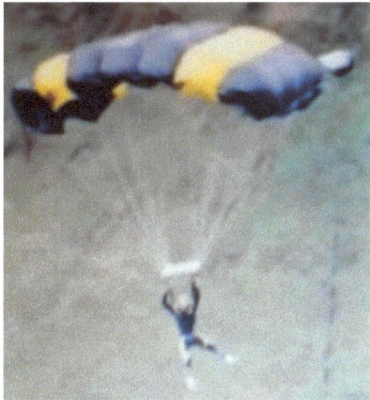

Vin Diesel leap beginning of XXX (Remote Intelligence)

Arrows   Psi paint by 1st 5th

KING ARTHUR starring Clive Owen

Christian Artefact II (view looking down into the center of the paint)

CANADIAN FORCES in Afghanistan 2011

Cdn troops Psi paint shows legs in V shape pattern, at bottom left, small but clear
Below are more vehicles RV from July 1st Canada Day celebrations, Edm Garrison.

Antennae & emote for troops

Color swath (center)

claw

Edmonton Garrison   Canada Day 2011

Air blade illusion RV

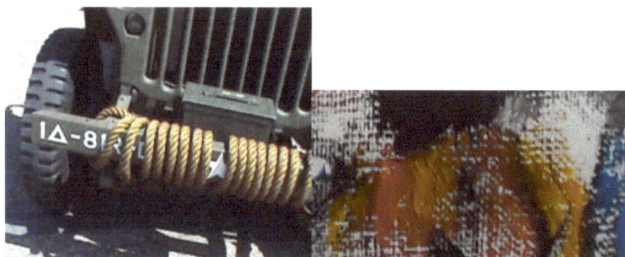

Ropes USA Artefactoid! Er, Jeep

Overlap RV: visual descriptive for guys off vehicle on ground

Tank

Q5 LEAP - Q5 LEAP - Spacetimelight notes July 2, 2011

To understand the subtle distinctions that occur with the layering effect of the story packets or encapsulations of information, we practice *discernment*.

To work on different security events at the same time, in an *holistic* manner.

Now, the paints also have the feature that they can shift a hyper shift directional and revolving so it's a continuously shifting visual frame of reference. Means the start of one object can be on the left of the page and then the rest at the other side entirely! It's motion sensitive, like a film that's shifting along… not just unfolding. That's the quantum light ingredient, particles AND waves are both present at Quantum levels when the subatomic or whatever title they use, physicists photo it during particle acceleration/smashing. Oh and also the reversible time arrow effect of quantum that's been documented to exist.

AMORPHOUS is another term that shows in the process of Quantum Psi; features continuously shifting, focus and cohesion and Psi packets can be 'held' as a visual precision and/or descriptive.

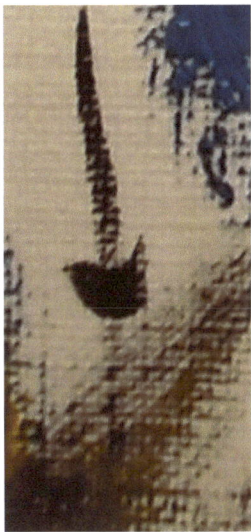

Divining Rod (white linear pattern lines, match to one I used)

1 Corinthians Chapter 13

13:1 "If I speak with the tongues of men and of angels, but do not have love, I have become a noisy gong or a clanging cymbal.

2. And if I have the gift of prophecy, and know all mysteries and all knowledge; and if I have all faith, so as to remove mountains, but do not have love, I am nothing.

...

13:13 "But now abide faith, hope, love, these three: but the greatest of these is love. "

Chapter 14 (page 412)

1 "Pursue love, yet desire earnestly spiritual gifts, but especially that you may prophesy.

2 For one who speaks in a tongue does not speak to men, but to God; for no one understands but in his spirit he speaks mysteries.

3. But one who prophesies speaks to men for edification and exhortation and consolation.

4. One who speaks in a tongue edifies himself, but one who prophecies edifies the church.

5. Now I wish that you all spoke in tongues, but even more that you would prophesy, and greater is one who prophesies than one who speaks tongues, unless he interprets, so that

the church may receive edifying.

...

22 So then tongues are for a sign, not to those who believe, but to unbelievers; but prophecy is for a sign, not to unbelievers, but to those who believe.

23. If there for the whole church should assemble together and all speak in tongues, and ungifted men or unbelievers enter, will they not say that you are mad

24. But if all prophesy, and an unbeliever or an ungifted man enters, he is convicted by all, he is called to account by all;

25. The secrets of his heart are disclosed; and so he will fall on his face and worship God, declaring that God is certainly among you.

26. What is the outcome then, brethren when you assemble each one has a psalm, has a teaching, has a revelation, has a tongue, has an interpretation. Let all things be done for edification. "

29 And let two or three prophets speak and let the others pass judgement

30 but if a revelation is made to another who is seated, let the first keep silent.

31 for you can all prophesy one by one, so that all may learn and all may be exhorted

32 and the spirits of prophets are subject to prophets

(I told you they do that make a distinction between prophecy and bad apples you don't just believe it all or reverse it all either, here you can see them advising discernment, ... it's prophecy/gift/quantum ... not YE GREATER THAN OTHERS PROPHETS ...but that said, there are gifted and non and some who just don'g believe. Etc. it's not instant godhead or evil Genie time... neither one. You people should try reading the Bible and listening and then heeding if you ask me. Your understanding of and application of Prophecy is sad. Well some are more attuned than others...

33 for God is not a God of confusion but of peace, as in all the churches of the saints.

Then 34 and 35 preach that 'women were not allowed to speak in the churches' ...so see Islam/ you are not alone, we reformed. The women are free to sing, chat dance smile talk chatter all they like ...we don't hold their mouths sewn ...that was an old old dictate and our society advances modernized and reformed. We did not stay like in those ancient times.

We allowed for FREEDOM PEACE PROSPERITY AND CHANGE: We talk. You need to let the women in with the men. Anything else is empty pretence and we are not doing islam over here. That's non negotiable.

RV in black & white
hang on a spell—
what's that Moses—
your

tablets

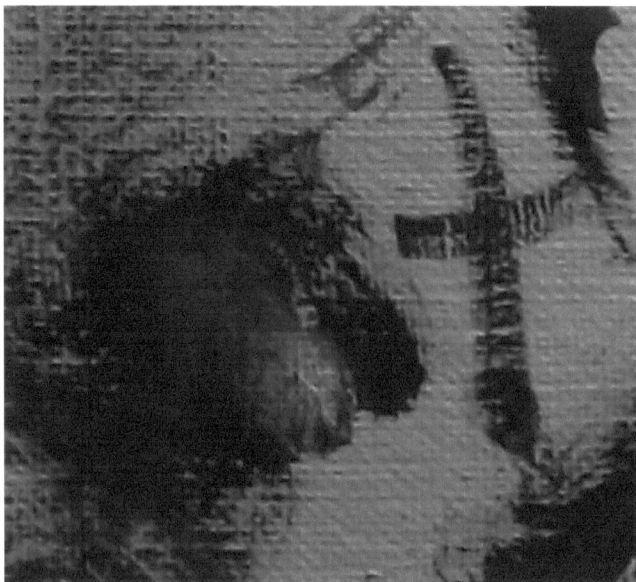

Spectral Military image, man with hat enlarged at right, above.

We

(here at Quantum Psi Hypershift 5ᵗʰ D Leap Time Tunnel remote viewing by 1ˢᵗ 5ᵗʰ trained by Military not Froggies OR Leprechauns!)

do changing code links the enemy just think they're following along but we follow their 'following' and it's pretty handy so keep up the good work, give the Helpful Aides Award to them!

CF-18 Trails Edmonton, Alberta wondrous Star Trail Views from Earth Side .

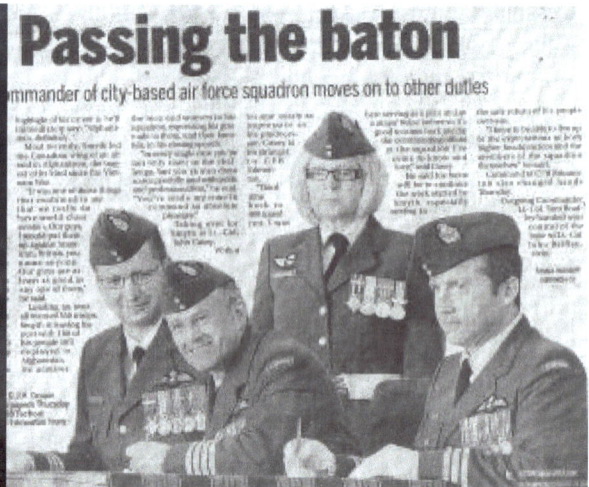

408 Tactical Helicopter Squadron — to Lt Col John Casey 2011

…hominid leap is a work in progress check back for more remarkable psi
www.nuts4mars.com

Psi training paint by 1st 5th, Quantum Stargate 2000

HEY watch out for them old cowboys—Steve McQueen did a movie called **tom horn** some cowboy they had him on trial for shooting some guy and he had nothing to do with it they just didn't like him and he was there outside minding his own business so finally he sneered 'yeah it was me' and they hung him for confessing. It was just him being a smart ass and they were just out to get him anyway. That was the last hanging in the Old West i think they said it was; they shut them down afterwards.

Here is another picked on Cowboy the songster

Willie Nelson

They had obama releasing a Mexican guy who raped/murdered a teen while they simultaneously hit us with a two punch of charging Willie Nelson for some personal pot stash belonging to his wife…. So ugly but that's what they did….just recently it's July 2011 and that's not a nice world anymore that's more like sharia. In their lands; takes 4 muslim men to witness a rape or the complaining victim gets stoned to death. Last year in eran the ayatoldya and his ilk upgraded to hanging one instead of the old goat's boy fave of stoning …. We need to rethink a few things - use ink swat what & when ever

To KEEP OUR FREEDOM as blessed is   -- if it came to it

Duke & Duchess of Cambridge

During a friendly romp in Canada and the USA, in the summer of 2011, here is the newly married to Kate, Prince William, now Duke of Cambridge, playing Polo and focusing on the end to successfully link to Q5 Leap Quantum Psi painting during their stay.

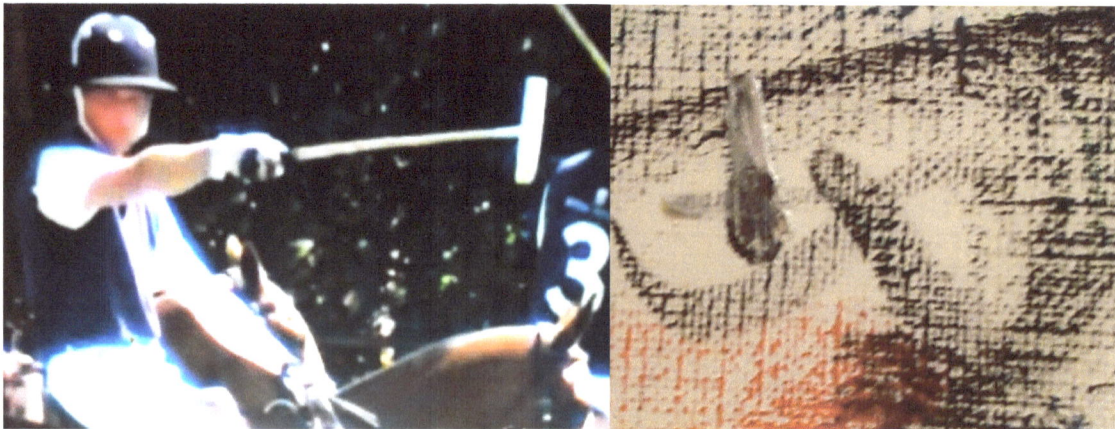

Note the horse's ear tips also caught in the Psi visual paint, just below the emote stick man image of the Royal, showing as a dark tracing over the brown coloring; the stick is done as a long white streak inside of which you can make out a long thin white visual, with the outermost white cross ending done 'as a streak across' it, as RV is often *descriptive* as well as visual. Then inside the greyish round under that white vertical you can see the image visual of a man, with an overlaid image of the grey hat brim with the white curved sides.

Psi paint by 1st 5th July 11th, 2011

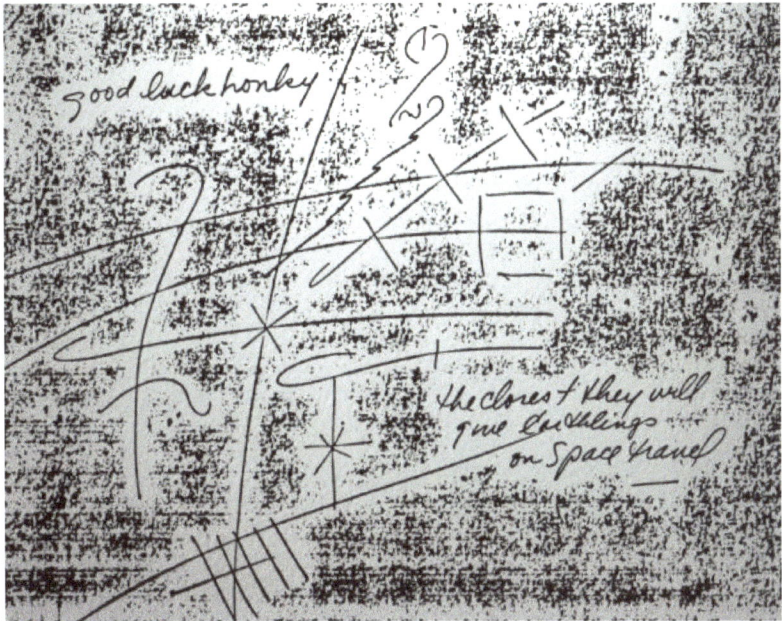

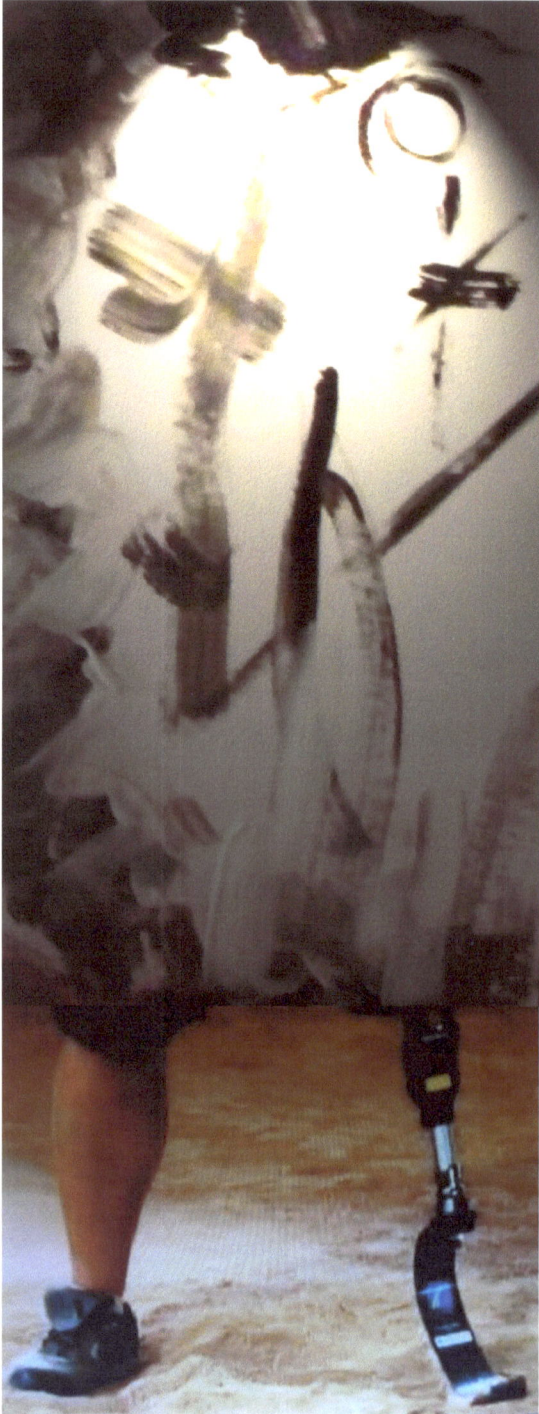

Wounded Warriors & Psi Paint

Lt-Col John Reiffenstein - new commanding officer CFB Edmonton, AB Canada

Tomahawk Cruise Missile

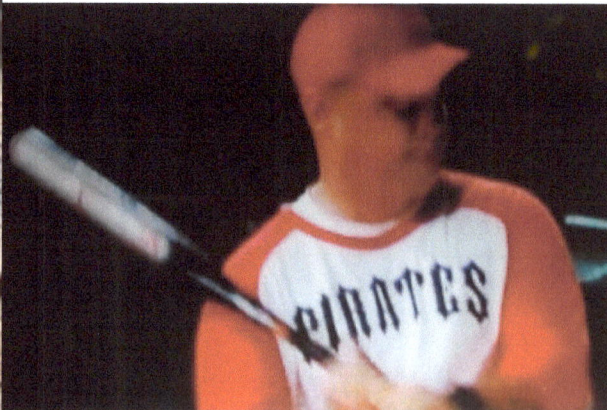

Babe Ruth

Both the Wounded Warrior ball player and Babe Ruth have silver bats in same time context, so the Psi painting at left and above, shows 2 bats in grey as a silver match.

Eddie Peoples, US Army Soldier thwarted Bank robbery single-handedly at Sarasota, Florida, USA much to the delight of the local Police.

US Army Sgt 1st Class Leroy Arthur Petry is the Medal of Honour recipient presented by Pres Obama, 2011, for catching a grenade, saving others' lives, and managing to stay alive.

Edmonton Sky Trails

Soyuz Russian Spacecraft

Soyuz Russian Space Craft (you can make out the image in the top right corner, looks a bit like a thermos) And below it on the ground is a phantom realism RV image of a Northern Canadian parachute on the ground; Psi Paint by 1st 5th early training CRV peaks, 2006, recruited by Pres Bush, to work on Counterterrorism and trained by Military using pc pixel psi release, intense, immersed, isolated and silent talk/rnm monitored, continuously accessed Psychic working Quantum Psi codes and skills.

Northern Canadian parachute on ground

Nostradamus & his Prophecies
by Edgar Leoni, page 179

61 ..."O Trojan blood! Mars at the port of the arrow.
Behind the river the ladder put to the fort,
Points to fire great murder on the breach."

62 "Mabus then will soon die, there will come
Of people and beasts a horrible rout:
Then suddenly one will see vengeance,
Hundred, hand, thirst, hunger when the comet will run."

007 James Bond, Daniel Craig- RV of blue eyed wolf
Secretly married the British actress Rachel Weisz

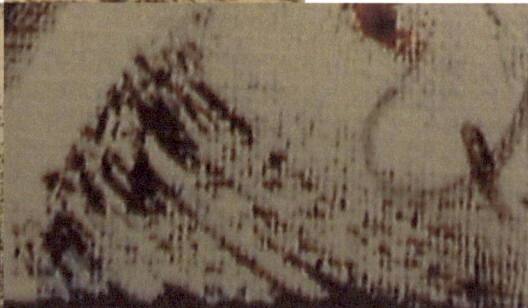

Mice on guard ... Safety is never superfluous ...

Mysterious photo of possible *Chupacabra* ⋯.

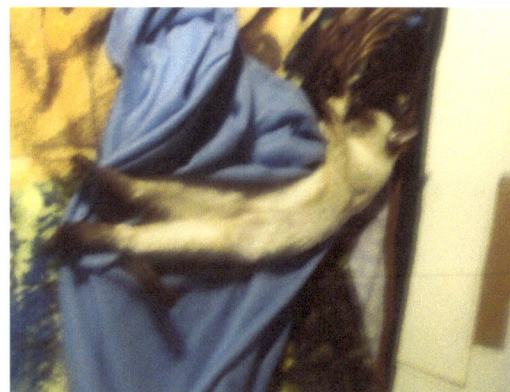

(it was kitty sleeping when she was small…)

Oh, he left, Gaddafi is on some tropical rich island like David Copperfield own; maybe he rented it, he rents it out you know, to whomever. See ya.

ARIVADARCI!

Gaddafi bugging out ....finally

Rick Hansen (Man in Motion World Tour) with slanted chair wheel, grey at far right above
Lit torch at 2010 World Olympics… inspirational for overcoming physical challenges.

Cops bike's wheels; troops & cops emotes

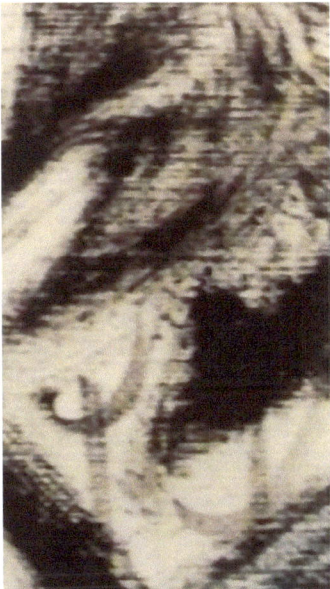

US Ambassador to Afghan, formerly to Iraq, Ryan Crocker

Libya - tanks RV 2011

Glock (Cop's Demo)

Sky Trails by CFB Edm AB

2011 Tomb of the Unknown Soldier USA; continuously guarded since Apr 6th 1948

Canadian Forces Base Edmonton, Alberta   ARTILLERY show Sept 5th, 2011

KIEFER SUTHERLAND and long gun   Sept 2011

*Note: extended arm with gun- pose in blue, at the top of the RV; it's a marker for his tv series '24'

AIM WEST SHOOT HIGH

troops on roof actually waving hi to 1ˢᵗ 5ᵗʰ the 'like a light house keeper' viewer

Cops RV theme - blue Knight's visor & wand

Quantum Psi - Bulls' horns with dark tips

CF - 18 HORNET

http://www.youtube.com/watch?v=cjek7QQbZP4&feature=related

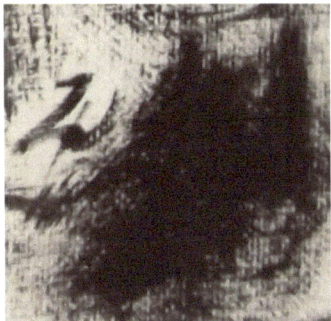

PHANTOM OPS

Sept 2011, visit by French Pres Nicolas Sarkozy and British PM David Cameron; LIBYAN youth's bravery and persistence resulting in a successful Revolution aiming for freedom along with a healthy dose of modernization, aided by a USA Tomahawk Cruise Missiles kick off and a sound pounding by NATO forces.

Libya 2011

perfect Puddings the Military wish list Kitty gift to 1ˢᵗ 5ᵗʰ

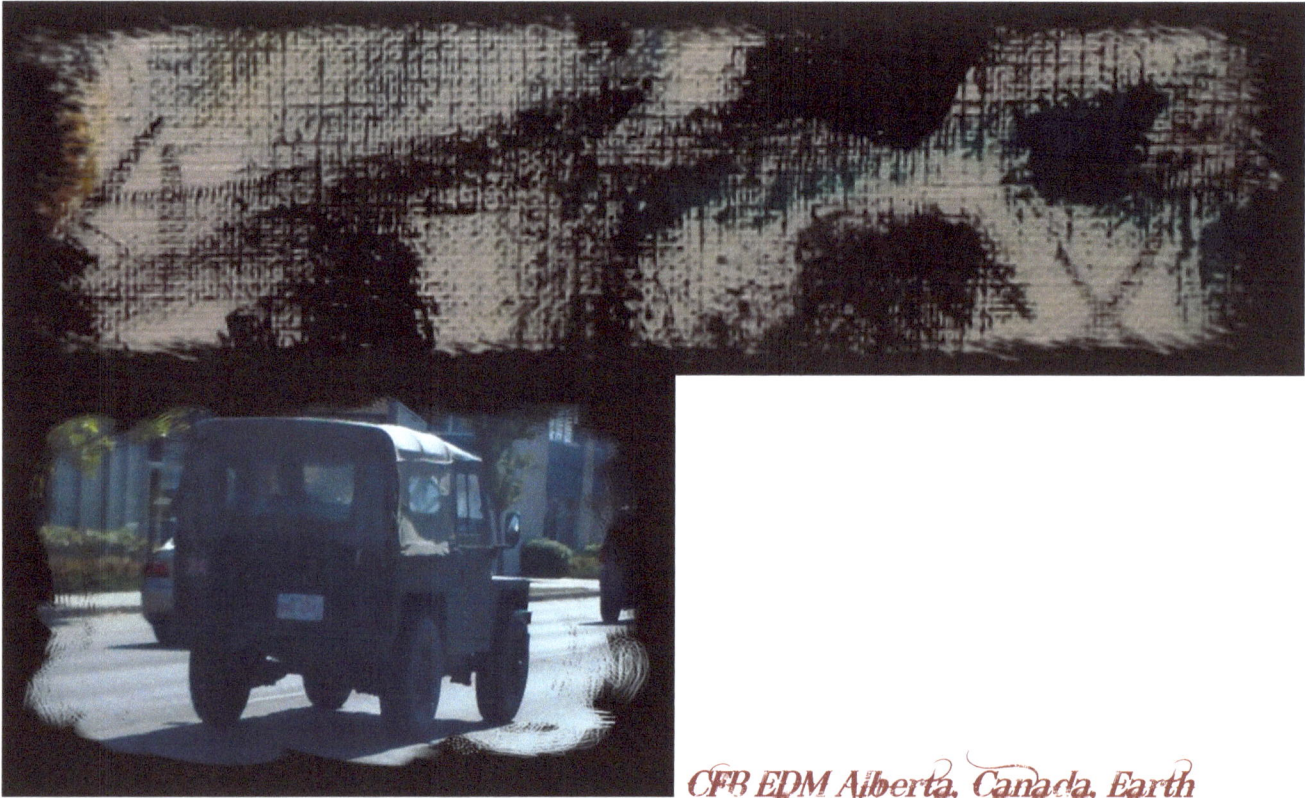

CFB EDM Alberta, Canada, Earth

British Terror Arrest

DINO HEAD & CLAW   Sept 2011

With assistance from NATO, successful Libyan Rebels in Bani Walid 2011

New York Ground Zero Cross; ancient Egyptian Chariot papyrus Remote View;

1st 5th also subscribes to the interpretation of the visuals as being indicative of a future

Development of SOLAR LAP TOPS the aim of the arrow tip makes a tangent with the orb.

Pre SEALS & some Fmr Marines & Trainer, Volunteer 22 years

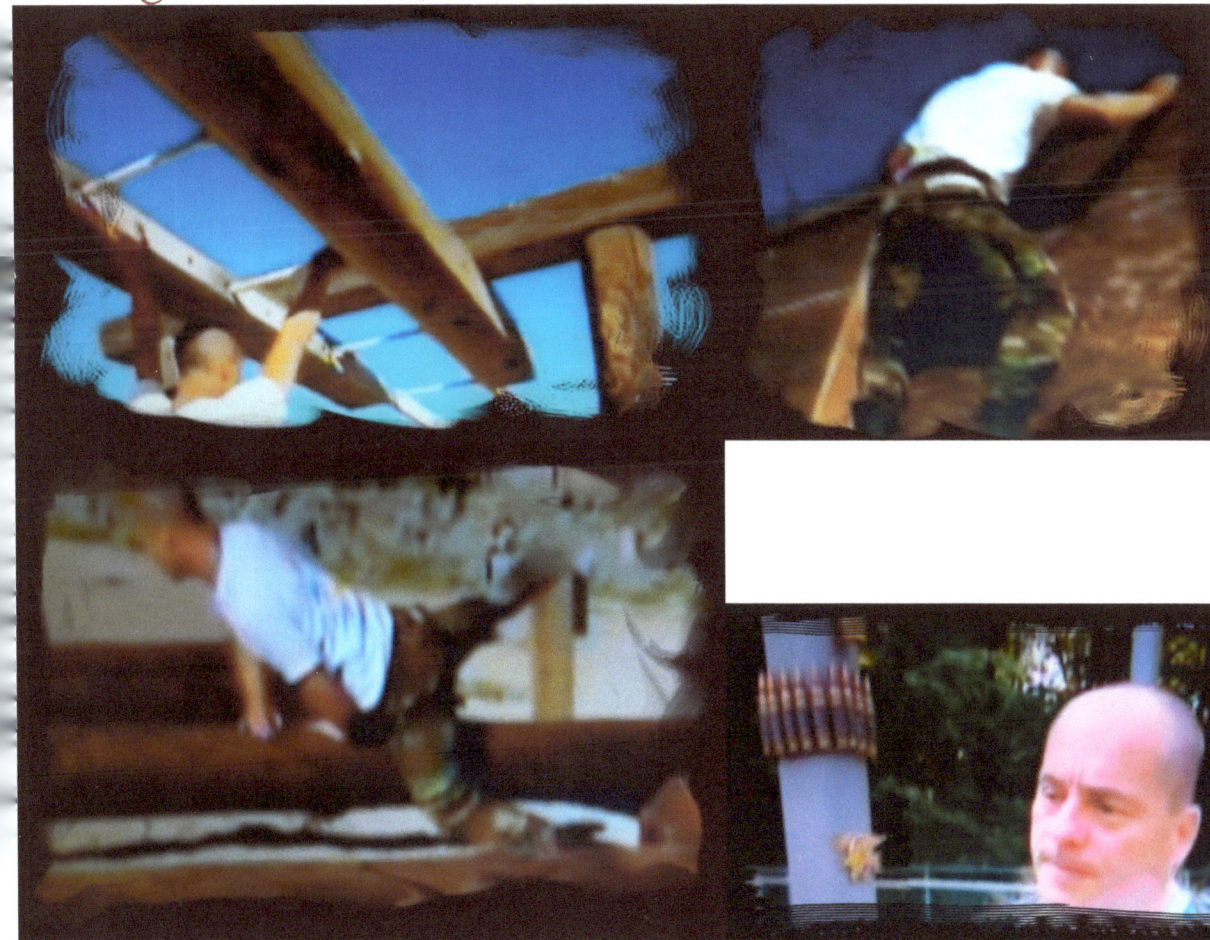

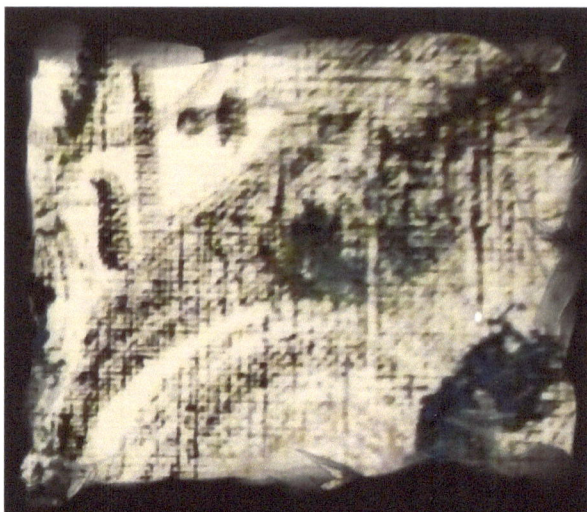

Trainer pre SEALS

Troops rolling over Quantum Psi with emote form, above at right

And the men were all faithful to their wives and lived happily ever after.

Why, just the other day there was this guy who was screwing his girlfriend, and just *yelling* out his wife`s name!

Charlie Sheen 'Violent Torpedo of Truth' Tour

In for a penny in for a pound…

www.ingramcontent.com/pod-product-compliance
Lightning Source LLC
Chambersburg PA
CBHW041425090426
42741CB00002B/38